A a	B b	C c	D d
E e	F f	G g	H h
I i	J j	K k	L l
M m	N n	O o	P p
Q q	R r	S s	T t
U u	V v	W w	X x
Y y	Z z		

Alphabetabum

THE NEW YORK REVIEW CHILDREN'S COLLECTION
NEW YORK

Alphabetabum

VERSES FROM A TO Z

COLLECTION OF RARE PHOTOS
AND ESSAY

Chris Raschka

Vladimir Radunsky

A a

Awkward Agnes Alexandra
Shows her ample ankles
Although her knees are grander.

Bb

Baby Beulah Bridget

Balances one big bow

But does not fidget.

Cc

Classy Cornelia Christine
Casts a cryptic countenance
And looks quite clean.

Dd

Dapper Duncan Dwayne

Doesn't dare sit down

Again.

Ee

Excellent Edwin Eugene
Executes each etude with ease,
If you know what I mean.

F f

Fabulous Freddie Fritz
Feels frankly foolish
Though his sailor suit fits.

Gg

Gifted Glenda Grace

Glows gorgeously with a grin

Half as wide as her face.

Hh

Happy Henrietta Hester
Holds her hands under a hat
That clearly impressed her.

I i

Itchy Irwin Isaac
Is inimitable, including
His stick.

J j

Jumpy Joanie Jewel

Just barely keeps the jitters

From jiggling her from her stool.

SAAZ S. Teller RINGPLATZ 42.

RINGPLATZ 42

Kk

Keen Kerry Keith
Keeps smiling
Through his teeth.

E. Montesi

ROMA

L l

Little Lucian Leroy

Likes licorice, although lollipops are his

Real joy.

M m

Merry Margo Maxine
Mistress of music
Manhandles the tambourine.

Nn

Naughty Norbert Newell
Feeds his horse on nothing but
Nicotine and gruel.

Oo

Ostentatious Oliver Owen

Often ogles obviously,

But he knows where he's going.

otograf Sørensen,
heatergade 2,
Næstved.

Pp

Pretty Penelope Pearl

Shows you with pockets like these that
She's a pretty special girl.

Sebastiana Palella
DIRETTORE G.CELSO

ACIREALE

Q q

Quiet Quentin Quint

Quite uniquely

Has conquered his squint.

Rr

Robust Rita Roxanne

Rakes rigorously

Whenever she can.

Ss

Salty Shelby Scott

Sings seasonal songs

Whether in season or not.

Roberts
STUDIOS

1254 FULTON ST.
683 FRESH POND RD.
BROOKLYN, N.Y.

T t

Terrific Tina Theresa

Touts tremendous tresses;

If you touch them, you'll displease her.

Uu

Uppity Ursula Uma
In umbrage, under her umbrella,
Unmans every rumor.

FORMATO VISITA

Virtuous Victor Vance

Is vaguely vainglorious

With his hands in his pants.

J. Schildkret $ BERTSCH

Ww

Wily Wesley Ward
Wields his wicked whip
When he walks without his sword.

Formato Gabinetto.

Xx

Excellent Axle Xavier

Expertly exercises

His best behavior.

Praha-Žižkov,
Sladkovského nám.
čís. 312.

Desky se pro další objednávky uschovají.

Číslo desky
Zvětšování obrazu.

Y y

Young Yolanda Yvette

Has a yearly yen

For an exotic pet.

Zz

Jazzy Zelda Zip
Oozes confidence with a hand
Upon her hip.

Fotograf v PÍSKU.

Stabilimenti
Fotografici
*Montesi
Emilio*
ROMA
CORSO VITT. EM. 199-201

SUCCURSALI
Corso Vitt° Em° 72
Torre Argentina, 32
Corso Vitt° Em: 238 240

Tutti in giardino

PHOTOGRA

Rue de
PLACE D'
CONSTAN

SCHMITT
v.
PRAZE
MALÁ STRANA
ČÍSLO 412.

PRAG
KLEINSEITE N° 412.

HASENBURG.

Are these children our great-great-great-grandparents?

I started collecting old photographs many years ago. I found them in flea markets, antique shops, sometimes just on the tables of street vendors: I found them in the United States, England, Italy, France, Spain, Portugal, Russia...

Every time I saw these small stacks, bound together with a plain rubber band or just scattered around in messy piles on the tables, I entered into this fantastic cardboard black and white and silver world, where I found myself surrounded by beautifully dressed ladies and gentlemen, their children and pets.

And if I turned these pieces of cardboard over, I'd see even more: coats of arms, medals, engraved names of photographers' studios, exotic-sounding addresses, elaborate ornaments—so much to look at.

It is difficult to tell now who the people captured in those photos were. But this thought occurred to me: If these photos were taken in the late-nineteenth or early-twentieth centuries, then the children in them could have been our great-great-great-grandparents! So we have an extraordinary chance to see what our great-great-great-grandparents looked like when they were children.

Some of them miraculously reappeared years later in flea markets or on the shelves of antique shops.

It took a long time and a lot of handling by strangers before they wound up with their new owners. They appeared in their new homes, no longer as beloved relatives or friends but more as guests, keeping a mysterious silence and refusing to give their names, unless one was found by accident on the back, written there by the careful hand of a previous owner.

People had their pictures taken infrequently back then. Only very important occasions merited photos—weddings, birthdays, long separations, etc.

Prints were costly: They were made by hand, one by one, and glued onto expensive thick cardboard with luxurious gold embossing on the back.

Usually whole families would go to the photographer's studio, where the photo artist (as they used to call themselves) carefully orchestrated the event. Slightly embarrassed, the subjects were arranged against rich backdrops, which were painted in oils and might depict anything from an expensively decorated interior to a picturesque countryside.

Everything and everybody was supposed to look perfect, better than in real life. That's why people put on their best clothes and tried to look significant. At the photographer's command they obediently froze in front of the camera, looking stiff. And that's how they remain forever and ever in these photos.

But did you notice how when we look at these small photos again and again the still figures come alive as they once were before they were frozen in time, blinded by the flash of an unknown photographer?

—Vladimir Radunsky

Per afflitti ala ricordo
Ottuma di Luvanigna

Fotograf v PÍSKU.

FORMATO VISITA

This book was made possible with the generous support of Baryshnikov Productions and the Andrey Goncharenko Foundation.

To all the unknown photographers whose marvelous photos appear in this book, and to those children whose extraordinary expressions they captured and brought to us.

To Misha. And to Anya, Sasha, Zheka, and Tsetsa.

THIS IS A NEW YORK REVIEW BOOK
PUBLISHED BY THE NEW YORK REVIEW OF BOOKS
435 Hudson Street, New York, NY 10014
www.nyrb.com

Library of Congress Cataloging-in-Publication Data
Raschka, Christopher.
Alphabetabum : an alphabet album / Chris Raschka, Vladimir Radunsky.
    pages cm
ISBN 978-1-59017-817-1 (hardback)
1. English language—Alphabet—Pictorial works—Juvenile literature. 2. Alphabet—Pictorial works—Juvenile literature. 3. Alphabet—Poetry. I. Radunsky, Vladimir. II. Title.
PE1155.R35 2014
421'.1—dc23
                    2014013271

ISBN 978-1-59017-817-1

Printed in the United States on acid-free paper.
10 9 8 7 6 5 4 3 2 1

VLADIMIR RADUNSKY

Vladimir Radunsky has published more than thirty books for children and received numerous awards, including several *New York Times* Best Illustrated Book Awards and Bologna's Critici in Erba. Some of his books have appeared on the *New York Times* best-seller list.

Driven by his strong conviction that the world where animals wear clothes, which we are familiar with from children's books, really does exist, Radunsky dedicates his spare time to creating fanciful clothes for large animals. His equestrian pants for racehorses, wedding dresses for boa constrictors, swimming trunks for hippos, slippers for elephants, etc., were exhibited as part of Milan Fashion Week and at the Palazzo delle Esposizioni in Rome.

CHRIS RASCHKA

Chris Raschka has written and/or illustrated more than sixty books for children, including *Yo! Yes?*, *Charlie Parker Played Be Bop*, *Mysterious Thelonious*, *Sluggy Slug*, *Five for a Little One*, *A Poke in the I*, and *The Hello, Goodbye Window*, and has received a Caldecott Honor, two Caldecott Awards, the Ezra Jack Keats Award, and five *New York Times* Best Illustrated Book Awards. He has knitted nine sweaters and one sock. Someday he hopes to knit another sock.

SELECTED TITLES IN THE NEW YORK REVIEW CHILDREN'S COLLECTION

ESTHER AVERILL
Captains of the City Streets
The Hotel Cat
Jenny and the Cat Club
Jenny Goes to Sea
Jenny's Birthday Book
Jenny's Moonlight Adventure
The School for Cats

JAMES CLOYD BOWMAN
Pecos Bill: The Greatest Cowboy of All Time

PALMER BROWN
Beyond the Pawpaw Trees
Cheerful
Hickory
The Silver Nutmeg
Something for Christmas

SHEILA BURNFORD
Bel Ria: Dog of War

DINO BUZZATI
The Bears' Famous Invasion of Sicily

MARY CHASE
Loretta Mason Potts

CARLO COLLODI AND FULVIO TESTA
Pinocchio

INGRI AND EDGAR PARIN D'AULAIRE
D'Aulaires' Book of Animals
D'Aulaires' Book of Norse Myths
D'Aulaires' Book of Trolls
Foxie: The Singing Dog
The Terrible Troll-Bird
Too Big
The Two Cars

EILÍS DILLON
The Island of Horses
The Lost Island

ELEANOR FARJEON
The Little Bookroom

PENELOPE FARMER
Charlotte Sometimes

PAUL GALLICO
The Abandoned

LEON GARFIELD
The Complete Bostock and Harris
Smith: The Story of a Pickpocket

RUMER GODDEN
An Episode of Sparrows
The Mousewife

MARIA GRIPE AND HARALD GRIPE
The Glassblower's Children

LUCRETIA P. HALE
The Peterkin Papers

RUSSELL AND LILLIAN HOBAN
The Sorely Trying Day

RUTH KRAUSS AND MARC SIMONT
The Backward Day

DOROTHY KUNHARDT
Junket Is Nice
Now Open the Box

MUNRO LEAF AND ROBERT LAWSON
Wee Gillis

RHODA LEVINE AND EDWARD GOREY
He Was There from the Day We Moved In
Three Ladies Beside the Sea

BETTY JEAN LIFTON
AND EIKOH HOSOE
Taka-chan and I

NORMAN LINDSAY
The Magic Pudding

ERIC LINKLATER
The Wind on the Moon

J. P. MARTIN
Uncle
Uncle Cleans Up

JOHN MASEFIELD
The Box of Delights
The Midnight Folk

WILLIAM McCLEERY
AND WARREN CHAPPELL
Wolf Story

JEAN MERRIL AND RONNI SOLBERT
The Pushcart War

E. NESBIT
The House of Arden

ALFRED OLLIVANT'S
Bob, Son of Battle: The Last Gray Dog of Kenmuir
A New Version by LYDIA DAVIS

DANIEL PINKWATER
Lizard Music

ALASTAIR REID AND BOB GILL
Supposing…

ALASTAIR REID AND BEN SHAHN
Ounce Dice Trice

BARBARA SLEIGH
Carbonel and Calidor
Carbonel: The King of the Cats
The Kingdom of Carbonel

E. C. SPYKMAN
Terrible, Horrible Edie

FRANK TASHLIN
The Bear That Wasn't

VAL TEAL AND ROBERT LAWSON
The Little Woman Wanted Noise

JAMES THURBER
The 13 Clocks
The Wonderful O

ALISON UTTLEY
A Traveller in Time

T. H. WHITE
Mistress Masham's Repose

MARJORIE WINSLOW
AND ERIK BLEGVAD
Mud Pies and Other Recipes

REINER ZIMNIK
The Bear and the People

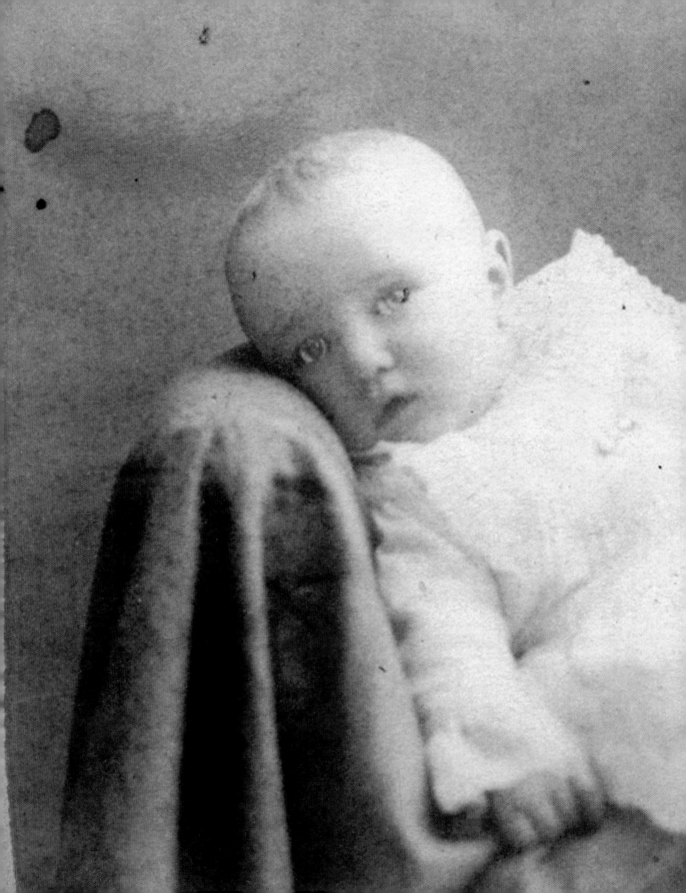